THE TRICK OF 511

THE POETRY IS BASED ON THE INDIA PENAL CODE 1860. IT COMPRISES OF SECTION 1 TO SECTION 511 OF THE INDIAN PENAL CODE.

ANKITA GUPTA

Copyright © Ankita Gupta
All Rights Reserved.

ISBN 978-1-63714-818-1

This book has been published with all efforts taken to make the material error-free after the consent of the author. However, the author and the publisher do not assume and hereby disclaim any liability to any party for any loss, damage, or disruption caused by errors or omissions, whether such errors or omissions result from negligence, accident, or any other cause.

While every effort has been made to avoid any mistake or omission, this publication is being sold on the condition and understanding that neither the author nor the publishers or printers would be liable in any manner to any person by reason of any mistake or omission in this publication or for any action taken or omitted to be taken or advice rendered or accepted on the basis of this work. For any defect in printing or binding the publishers will be liable only to replace the defective copy by another copy of this work then available.

To my beloved family who hold my hands in every situation.

To my friends who are the shine which never leaves apart its jewels.

To teachers & Mentors who deepen my roots in the soil of light & knowledge.

To my school & college who made me firm to stand and face the dense forest of the world.

The book is dedicated to everyone who wants to learn the Indian Penal Code, 1860 in a poetic style.

A book is not just a combination of pages & words but it a feeling of light, knowledge & love.

Contents

Foreword — vii

Preface — ix

Acknowledgements — xi

THE TRICK OF 511

About The Author — 45

Foreword

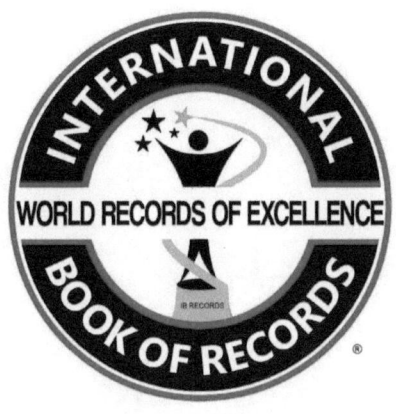

RECORD HOLDER

ANKITA GUPTA

The Poetic Book "The Trick of 511" has set a WORLD RECORD of "LONGEST LAW POETRY" by Ankita Gupta on 29th October 2020. She has compiled section 1 to section 511 of The Indian Penal Code, 1860 and took 5 Days to complete it.
- By International Book Records.

Preface

The journey of the poem was not easy, yet neither was it difficult. The Indian Penal Code, 1860 has been the official criminal code of India, comprises a total 511 sections however the author has rediscovered the draft and assembled the sections in a poetic approach.

The readers can amplify the sections in poetry which will enhance the learner to grasp sections in an easier manner with imagination.

The idea behind the poem is to change the way of learning things in a better way instead of going with a traditional method. The poem consists of short stories in it which will increase your mind's eye.

I hope the poem will help you to learn the sections of the Indian Penal Code in an easier way.

Open the book with love & pleasure. Light up your heart, spread the happy smile, glow your face with a loving smile. Twinkle your eye, give the book a way to the Mariana trench of your heart.

Acknowledgements

An author is nothing without its reader. The first and the foremost praise goes to the readers.

Who makes authors write awesome books. Readers are the ink to the author's pen.

Well said, to accomplish something it requires the efforts of many people and this work is also one of them. It's very difficult for an author like me to express gratitude as some valuable emotions can't be expressed but can be feeled.

Let eyes speak for some time, let the emotion flow in you. Let this silent love flow in all, I thank you all.

THE TRICK OF 511

It's a clear sky when criminals are penalised,

Yes, the Indian Penal Code describes,

From section 1 to 5 talks about territorial land,

The punishment including the land of nature,

The water of seas & maritime zones,

The offence committed within & beyond,

From any place of any citizen,

Whether it may be netizen of India,

YET YET YET,

There are special provisions for the heroes and heroines of land, air & sea.

(The poet is indicating heroes and heroines of land, air & sea to soldiers in army, airforce and navy)

Roses are grown in land or dreamland,

Let's talk about general explanation of our motherland,

From section 6 to 52(A) of the Indian Penal Code,

Yes! Yes! Yes!,

It comply of codes of every act,

It's a wonder book of crimes,

It has the compassion to hear all,

Whether it maybe male or female,

In any number,

Plural or singular,

Of any age,

Yet Yet Yet

Here a person is also a company or association,

From any community,

It can be from the servant of motherland

(the poet indicates servant of motherland to government employees)

Repealed Repealed Repealed

Section 13, 15 & 16 are repealed,

Hail Hail Hail

The wordbook of crime revealing the court of justice,

The judge, the Public servant, and many officers of Justice of land,

The attachment of its towards the ground are immovable,

Each & every particular aspect is punishable

that comes under unlawful act,

Punishment to every wrong gain, dishonesty, fraudulent,

The innocents are trapped as they have the reason to believe righteously.

Whoa Whoa Whoa the Story of King's Son began

It addresses the right of possession of Property,

Oh, it can punish you if you try to imitate someone to get treasures,

Yes! You will be punished for counterfeit,

Haha! You can be trapped by charter or machine tape of the Queen or King,

(the poet indicates charter means document, machine tape means electronic record)

The treasure pawns are kept hidden, the liar who will bring it up by malicious way will soon be trapped by the Lord of Justice.

(the poet indicates Treasure pawns means Valuable security)

The happiness in the face when the criminals are punished,

But it's the time to choose the successor of the King,

The WILL has arrived yet the Son has failed to act the responsibilities,

Created illegal omissions with his companion with all their knowledge and intention,

Yet, no one can be left or hidden from the Lord of Justice,

The crime book declares them criminals on the charges of the same offence.

Yet Yet Yet

It was found that the Son of the King committed more offences,

The Lord screamed the Son and declared section 34 of the Indian Penal Code,

The Son voluntarily declared himself felon and he disarmament himself the rest of his life.

The tragic story ends even though the Indian Penal is so far.

The clouds are shatter,

screaming to my ears,

And shedding tears to the land,

The law of crime is juggernaut spreaded in local law,

Any illegal act injuries to body is forbidden in the claw of law,

No life can be harmed and no death can be saved if you are wrong and the law of crime ruled land of law.

Still Still Still

If you are a good person and have good faith in your act nothing is a crime.

Hidden doors are now open,

Punishments are now revealed,

The code has decoded,

The Indian Penal Code has come to section 53 to section 75,

The mortal punishment begans,

The sentence of Death is marked,

Rigorous life imprisonment & solitary confinement are described,

Repealed Repealed Repealed

Section 56, 58, 59, 61 & 62 are repealed,

A few punishments are amount to fine,

Yet, if you are incapable of paying the amount,

you would lead to imprisonment for a certain time long.

It may bond you with theories of punishment to bring up reformation in you.

Everything in life has certain merits and demerits for you,

Indeed, the book of law has exceptions for you,

From section 76 to section 106 of the Indian Penal Code.

Our land excuses one if there is mistakes of facts,

but no excuse is given to mistakes of law.

The Judicial acts, acts by unsound person & by minor child, accidents, Private defence, Trifling acts, absences of criminal mind are never bound to punishment,

As these acts are done in good faith.

The mastermind of the game of law is to take free-consent of the other to be free from all liabilities,

YET YET YET

If consent is by fraudulent,

under fear or misconception,

by an intoxicated person,

or the one who is unable to understand the depthness of nature & its consequences,

These misrepresentations lead to penalty.

The sun has now brighten up in the blues,

With a wonderful rainbow in skies,

Here we come up with a new chapter,

From section 107 to section 120 of the Indian Penal Code,

The one who instigate or provoke,

The one who is the man behind the clouds,

Yes, it's the abettor.

The abettor can be one or two or many,

But liability is same on each,

The offence is with intention & conspiracy,

An illegal omission by one behind the scene,

It's not just by words,

But by conduct too,

Abetment has forms of doing act,

By facilitating an assistance to another,

STILL STILL STILL

If you are saved from getting killed,

Then the abettor behind the scene will be still in the jail,

Behind the bars or maybe with extra fine as per facts of the case.

The Punishment will be on the act of the abettor,

Alas! Sometime it may lead to the sentence of death,

Or imprisonment in jail.

Let open up the window of your home,

Let's focus on the hidden plan inside you,

The secret which has now in the vision,

Yes, let's discuss the section 120A & 120B of the Indian Penal Code,

The conspiracy backing the crime,

The agreement which is illegal,

And done by illegal means is immaterial,

If the crime is committed,

You will be penalised,

With death,

Or imprisonment,

And if your luck is good,

As your conspiracy is in foresee mood,

You will be imprisonment for a particular term,

And will be set-free that is confirmed.

The skies are thundering,

Offence are increasing,

People are waging war against the state,

It's not the right time to show your traits.

Oh yes, we are certainly illustrating section 121 to section 130 of the Indian Penal Code.

The war is never the solution of the problem,

We need the peace of discussion to solve some,

The action you take to assault the state or,

Waging a war against them,

Either by words, sign, showing disaffection, performing negligence

Or by aiding the prisoners to set free by rescuing leads towards penalty.

The wind is blowing high,

The heroes & heroines are cool,

(Hereby heroes & heroines will be called as heroes by the poet)

We are talking about section 131 to section 140 of the Indian Penal code.

Seducing our heroes is not right,

You are inviting yourself to fight,

Which led you to be penalised.

The intention may go wrong of any, maybe of our heroes,

If they found as wrong doer,

This will lead to the chance to be penalised.

Repealed Repealed Repealed

Section 138A is repealed.

The heroes are unique,

You can't imitate them intentionally and join the troop,

Has it led to punishment for you.

As bad habits are awful,

Today we will talk about unlawful,

True, we have reached the next chapter of Indian Penal Code,

From section 141 to section 160 it talks about offence against public tranquility,

It starts from unlawful assembly,

Beings its member you will be liable for punishment,

Society will led you to be banishment,

Creating a riot or fear is awful,

You can be guilty lawful,

If found in five,

Causing harm to the peace will be deprived,

The curve of your act,

Can led to riot,

This will drive you to prejudice,

And may cause to affray,

Which will lead to punishment & fine to your wonderful day.

Be genuine, be yourself,

It's time to relate public servant,

Beginning from section 161 to 171 of the Indian Penal Code.

Repealed Repealed Repealed

Section 161, 162, 163, 164, 165, 165A are repealed.

The book of penal does not save anyone,

From wrongful act done,

Disobeying law,

You can be catch up by law's claw,

Bidding for property & Fraudulent,

misrepresentation of being a public servant

Will grab you to imprisonment.

Rights are my new flight,

Where I can flew high in the sky,

My vote, is now your new stand,

As it's my duty to elect the right,

Let's talk about offence relating to elections,

Section 171A to section 171I of the Indian Penal Code.

I can stand,

You can stand,

But win with genuine not by bribery,

Exercise it freely not by undue influence,

Get the winning position by the true facts,

Not by false declaration,

Enjoy your rights without illegalization.

Running from difficulties is not a choice,

Excuse from law is of no joy,

And absconding from summon is penalised,

If you are neglecting the charter, be ready to apologize.

(the poet indicates charter means document)

Here, we are learning section 172 to section 190 of the IPC.

(The poet is denoting IPC as Indian Penal Code)

Multiform beware has its not a fiction,

But a book of law,

Punishment will be on,

False will not stay long,

You need to be truthful throughout.

Refusing to stay on your point,

Be ready with a ballpoint.

Rising up a barrier for servant of motherland

(the poet indicates servant of motherland to government employees)

Is not a good stand.

Servants of motherland bidding for yourself should not be your demand,

Bidding by others who are denied by law is not a good implant,

You both will be punished at first glance.

Hail Hail Hail

Aiding the servant of motherland is like a lending a hand,

If you are in a bond to lend a hand yet have omitted, be ready for a slam.

Your day will be bad if you high-hat the charter of the servant of motherland,

The punishment will arise at the tip of your nose as it commands.

Thinking to get rid of the servants of motherland,

Planning to threaten them firsthand,

Restrict yourself in your land,

Otherwise you will be grabbed,

In the demand of penalty land.

Life is full of mystery,

Tell me something about your history,

Let's move to the next chapter of IPC,

From section 191 to section 229.

Sway the verdict in the court,

Move them to the new boat,

Provide them with a forged proof,

Create your own mystery of roof,

YET YET YET

You are not under good approved,

The forgery has been disproved,

With this truth,

You are invited to blues.

Things are still kept hidden,

Silence are rising there voice,

The mystical hat is moving around like a black night,

The night is so long that it kills the rat,

(The poet is indicating Documents as rat in the text)

The killer is so strong,

Characterizing itself in multiforms,

The illicit blood falls on the ground,

The ground is claimed for the wrong,

The law has solved the mystery of fraudulent belongings,

The secrets are now revealed,

The Justice of Crime has arrived in the court,

To imprison the fraudulent man.

(The poet indicates both man & woman as man in the text)

DON'T DON'T DON'T

Try to conceal the culprit,

By taking offerings.

Repealed Repealed Repealed,

Section 216B is repealed.

LISTEN LISTEN LISTEN

The Servants of Motherland the notice is for you,

If it uncovers the mastermind as you for framing dishonest charter,

Acting contrary to law,

Bringing up omission,

Escaping from law,

Resisting any person,

Or find disobeying the law you will be chewed,

By the lord of justice.

Repealed Repealed Repealed,

Section 226 is repealed.

Not them but by you,

If found insulting will be in blues.

Yet Yet Yet

Some revelation is a rejection,

In the eyes of law,

If found violating the identity of the vulnerable you will be in law's claw,

Here, we end this chapter by section 229 of personation of the law.

Magics are shown in shows,

Joker makes jokes in the circus,

Today we will learn about Offences Relating to Coin and Government Stamps,

It starts with section 230 and ends in section 263A,

It bring ups the term coin,

With that I remember a important point,

Real lifes magic can be a illusion,

A fake to counterfeit the real substance.

Any foul play with the treasure is nuisance.

(The poet denotes treasures as coins)

You can be liable for damages.

Whosoever is fraudulently removing the engrave from the charter,

Liable for such behavior,

Under the Indian Penal Code treasurer.

Scams are high,

Fraudulent are in skies,

From chapter twelve,

Offences Relating to Weights and Measures,

False weight,

False measure,

Be aware,

Your chance are in air,

Lord of Justice is thundering,

Be ready for liability.

Creating fears in the mind,

Lets learn how to decline,

The offence affecting the Public Health, Safety, Convenience, Decency and Morals in crime,

From section 268 to section 294A of the IPC are defined

Found guilty for public nuisance in vicinity,

Spreading vicious disease is not divinity,

Disobedience to quarantine rule is not your masculinity,

Adulteration of drugs, foods & drinks are asininity,

Dealing with noxious food & drinks are stupidity,

Stinking the public water is blameworthy.

Vigilant Vigilant Vigilant

People of our surrounding be vigilant,

If found making noxious atmosphere,

Or playing a roadrashing on a road clear,

Shall be liable for forfeiture.

Life is precious,

Negligence is vicious,

Any unsafe act is contagious,

Your lives are in dangerous,

Deceiving is not righteous,

Risking someone's life treacherous,

Placing pebbles in one's way ungenerous,

Laxness in unlike creature iniquitous,

Constant public nuisance is mendacious,

Void Void Void

Obscene books, objects, acts & songs are suspicious,

Raffles in any office are malicious.

Gods & Goddess are prayed,

Don't use them has trade,

Let's move our train,

In the world of Indian Penal Code rail,

The city of offence has arrived,

The room of offence are opened,

From section 295 to section 298

Objects are offences relating religion,

Injury will cause if insult took base,

Outrage on any beliefs are debase,

Hassling the religious gathering are unpraised,

Injuring anyone's feelings in funeral ceremonies are likely to be disgrace,

Don't utter any deliberate words that harm the courteousness.

Enjoy each and every small things in life,

As we are unaware the arrival of death,

Let's learn something new in life,

From IPC section 299 to section 377.

The massacre as arrived,

The killer has shown up the face,

Its illegal to erase,

(The poet indicates to erase as to 'kill a person')

With a intention and knowledge disgrace,

Don't be happy for your footpace,

As you have snatched the life of grace,

You will be held responsible,

In the eyes of jurisprudence.

Death by negligence are chargeable,

Say no to offence which are dangerous,

Dowry deaths are punishable.

Alert Alert Alert

Abettors don't be hidden,

The power of law is everywhere,

In case you are the abettor,

Be ready to be punishable.

Alas! Save the apathetic,

Life is full of emphatic,

Don't measure your life and death,

Enjoy each day,

Don't attempt to kill your way.

Your path is yours,

be your hero,

Path maybe full of hurdles or villains,

Be Careful the thugs are on its way,

Show them your toughness,

And apply punishment on them.

Be responsible,

Be ethical in your choice,

Let's talk about the section 312,

It sings a sad song of a mother & its unborn child,

The death of miscarriage is unbearable,

The baby that is unborn is nondurable,

The society is so prejudice,

That it lives its child,

To die in the air,

To put an end to,

Some are so evil,

Cause a distressing survival,

Oh Lord! Save the mankind,

From such sinful people,

Who hurts another living being,

Just for their mean,

By causing heinous act,

Uses force,

Purposely intercourse.

Shame on the evil eye,

Who looks upon you with a dark connection.

(The poet indicates Dark Connection as Voyeurism)

Lord of Justice help!

Kill the black shadow,

Who follows,

Catch the rapacious who abduct just for pleasure,

The Justice Protector bring up the black faces,

Who exploit our nation's pride,

Who plays foul games and moves away inside.

Not just the outsider, but be aware of the insider.

It feels,

When the bond maker,

Ruin there everlasting nods,

Still containing physical intimacy by forcing the partner,

Grab them in law's claw.

In the rule of Justice lord,

No Servants of Motherland can hook up illicitly inside the door.

Open the eyes,

Listen to the cries,

Can you hear them,

Who are screaming for help,

No ears heard,

No eyes reflect,

Yes, you are right,

I am talking about the gang rape,

Punishments are forced,

Yet Yet Yet

The crime is still on,

There need to be a change,

A change for better society,

A change for you & me,

A change for the world,

Who loves each one of us.

Still Still Still

There are some dark shadow who are insane from brain,

And repeat the same dark illicit act of rape,

Who doesn't even leave the innocent living creature of nature.

(The poet indicates creature as animals and other living beings)

Elders have advised,

You are born twice,

One with respect,

Other with money,

As this world is ruled by currency,

The very chapter comes to mind is offence against the Property,

The arrival is from section 378 and departure is to section 462 of IPC.

Someone has said, Money rules over all relationships.

The world has changed,

Honesty has disappeared,

Thefts are taking place,

The most emotional weapon are raised,

Yes, Blackmails have made a base,

(The poet indicates blackmails as extortion)

The power of money had made innerspace,

People are forced to commit theft,

It has many names,

You can call it a despoil, or plunder claim,

People smash and run,

There no execution without a plan,

Chastising are in there horoscope withstand,

Dark assemblies are the talk of past command.

Here comes a new route of homeland,

It shows the path of trust,

But if you went through distrust,

You will be liable for three years unjust.

It is said, friends are made with trust,

If you break the promise of past,

The enemy of ours will laugh out a lot,

Yes, you will breach the law of trust,

The trust has many roles,

And creates more relationship,

Like a master & his servant,

The trust still remains the same.

Well said, Whatever you have earned,

With theft will soon fade away.

The capital possessions earned by smash & grab are ceased to be stolen grey,

The property earned by underhand way,

Shall be a way to imprisonment.

SCAM SCAM SCAM

Cheating leads beating from clan,

Let's apply section 420 in the line,

Bogus in the game or in the life,

Shall be liable for punishment,

Mischief causing lost to amount of fifty,

I love my money lofty,

Yet Yet Yet

Mischief with living creature is not tolerated,

Found injured for mischief will be imprisoned for unrated.

Still Still Still

The mischief doesn't end here,

The story of sea is yet to come in the sphere,

The goons are ready here,

Surrounds you from everywhere,

For the treasure cheer.

Be Alert Be Alert

The Pirates are over all,

Land, Air or Sea,

Looking after the property,

Pirates of land are trespasser,

Be Alert Be Alert

They can enter in your land,

For some delicious brand,

Be Alert all the time,

Has they are only concern about dime,

They can break,

They can bring an end to your life gate.

Some may be hidden in the dark world,

Be Alert from there underworld,

They can hidden for a pearl,

Yet, don't be afraid schoolgirl,

(The poet here in the line is not meant to discriminate against schoolgirls. A fear can occur in a schoolboy too who can be afraid and the sense of fear is not limited to any category it can be even you & me and everyone in the world, everyone has some sense of fear if not in real world but then definitely it can be in your dreamland.)

The law of Justice is here,

Can exceed the punishment upto 10 years.

Be afraid Dark Shadow,

You will be punished for your sin show.

Good planning is liked by everyone,

But the wicked love forgery one's.

Yes, we are talking about Offences Relating to Documents

And to Property Marks,

Fake charters are released by evils,

Don't worry there punishment is of different level,

Alert Alert Alert

If you have forge documents be alert,

You will he held liable,

If shown it up as verifiable.

Never Never Never

Dishonestly try to hurt the sentiment of people,

Otherwise your punishment will extend to seven years.

Repealed Repealed Repealed

Section 478 & section 480 are repealed.

A sign that is used to show the ownership,

Is being imprint by a trick,

Don't fall on in it so quick,

As it may cause you a big hit.

Fraud Fraud Fraud

Your currency may be fraud,

The coins & notes you have earned by blood,

May be fraud,

Remember from where you have got,

The offender will be caught,

With the help of legal law,

If found using fraudulent affluence,

Shall be punished for imprisonment for assurance.

Repealed Repealed Repealed

The next chapter on the crime is repealed.

Section 490 and section 492 are repealed.

Yet Yet Yet

Don't ignore the helping hand,

Agreed, section 491 is a supporting stand,

It helps the weak, unsound mind to rise there ends.

(The poet has indicated the term 'ends' as economic term 'ends' which means supply their wants)

Distance may end,

But Love never ends,

The day it ends, is the end of the world,

Somethings always remains sacred & pure,

Still some has blues in their world,

The world has changed its afterworld,

Let's talk about offence related to conjugal bond,

The bond is tie between section 493 to section 498 of IPC land,

Deceiving from the side of a man,

Inference a woman to cohabit as a couple can,

Sin Sin Sin

It is a sin to marry another guy,

(The poet indicates guy as an individual)

In the time of your current marriage life,

Any deceiving done in marriage ceremony the problem may arrive,

The lord of justice has direct the section 497 has no more alive,

Be aware ladies,

This section 498 is for your studies,

If found a illicit relationship with buddies,

(The poet is indicating buddies as men in this text)

You will be imprisoned as descripted.

The world has changed,

But mentality is still the same,

Totally agreed the cruelty of husband & its relatives are still on its base,

Yes, we are talking about section 498A.

Abuse abuse abuse

The world has left no choice to abuse,

The gossips are on,

You and me are the part,

Yes, we are talking the chapter of life,

The section of defamation drive,

Any act that engraves a defamatory matter in a broadwide,

Of a person is a defamatory crime.

Let's move to a connected chapter of crime,

Let's learn section 503 to section 510 of IPC time,

It says harming the reputation of one is a crime,

Consciously insulting is a breach of divine,

Foul play to public is a conduct of public tranquility sign,

Inducing anyone in the name of god is a crime,

Don't fall in, it's a waste of time.

Cautions people cautions,

In case caught you with a gesture or a word humiliating a woman's respect,

You will be imprisoned for an inhuman affect.

Evil doing is never accepted,

A person who is drunk always tresspasses,

In this way the individual is never greeted,

Yet, the person is still never been neglected,

From the eyes of intellect.

(The poet indicates intellect as Indian Penal Code in this text)

Welcome Welcome Welcome

You have reached the final destination,

The last chapter of the poem,

And the last page of the law of crime,

Lets learn section 511 of the IPC this time,

The law defines when one is attempting to crime,

Is an wartime,

The meantime is the expression of the attempt sign,

This attempt is committed offence under this line,

And its punishable with imprisonment for life,

Or sometimes according to the case file.

Let's say goodbye.

.

About The Author

Let the knowledge shower on you, let your brain take the roots. Let the light ripen you with the knowledge of growth.

A Law Student, currently in B.A.LL.B third year from Progressive Education Society Modern Law College affiliated to Savitribai Phule Pune University.

The main aim of Ankita, is to bring this poem to fascinate and grow interest in learning among students. She meant there are many ways to learn difficult subjects. Her approach towards India Penal Code was a bit different but unique in itself. She rediscovered the charter or the law in a poetic fashion.

Her passion to learn, imagine & feel the things made a difference from others. Her empirical approach to make things pure & simple has made Indian Penal Code easier for students or any learner who approaches for knowledge.

When you speak up, it's your voice. But when you stand for others it's your power of love for them.

www.ingramcontent.com/pod-product-compliance
Lightning Source LLC
LaVergne TN
LVHW041546060526
838200LV00037B/1167